# Wind
# and Rain

## Adria F. Klein

DOMINIE PRESS
Pearson Learning Group

ISBN  0-7685-1516-5

Printed in Singapore

4 5 6 7 8  07 06

Dominie
Press
Pearson Learning Group

1-800-321-3106
www.pearsonlearning.com

# Table of Contents

I like the wind. I can fly my kite.

The wind can be strong.
It can push over houses
and hurt the land.

The wind can be gentle.
It makes the flags fly
and the clothes dry.

I like the rain.

I can splash in the puddles.

The rain can be strong.
It can make the dirt move
down the hills.

The rain can be gentle.
It can make the grass green
and the trees grow.

Wind and rain are part of our world.

# Picture Glossary

flags:

kite:

grass:

puddles:

# Index